AND GOD SAID...

A Rhymed Account of Creation

CHANDA D. WEBB

OAK & WEBB PRESS™

And God Said...

Before the world had shape or sound,
Before the stars were spun around, Before
green grass, fruit and trees, Before fish swam
in the open seas,

There was a voice both strong and true-
Creation waited for what God would do.

And God said,

Let there be light, and light filled
space, the darkness moved and gave it
place.

God saw the light was good to see,
And kept it separate carefully.

He named the light the time of Day,
and the darkness Night, when light
went away.

There was evening then morning
came. The first day was formed and
given its name.

And God said,

Let there be a vault so high and wide-
A mighty stretch from side to side.

The waters parted by his word, above
and under all was stirred.

Some stayed below, some rose up high
and the vault between, God called it sky.

Evening came then morning new, God
called it good on day two.

And God said,

Waters I had made stay in one place,
and the dry ground, I call land, be
separate in its space.

The waters pulled back, dry land showed,
the Earth stood firm where water once
flowed.

The green plants sprang from the soil below, with each seed knowing how it ought to grow.

The land obeyed just as it should and the third day, God called it good.

And God said,

In the sky bring forth two great lights,
The Sun to rule the day, and the Moon
to rule the night.

Their steady paths would guide each day,
And mark the months along the way.

They will serve as signs for one and all, to mark Winter, Summer, Spring, and Fall.

And stars were made and planets too, day four was complete- both bright and new.

And God said,

Let the sea be filled with living things,
and the sky be covered with soaring
wings.

Then sea and sky with life were stirred,
each one created by His Holy Word.
From fin to feather, all alive, God blessed
His creatures on day five.

And God said,

Let the land produce creatures all to
roam, the wild, the tamed, to call Earth
their home.

The lions strong, the horses fast.
The tiny ant that crawls right past.
The cow, the sheep, the giraffe so tall,
God made them good, He made them all.

Then God said,

In our image, let's make mankind, a
heart to love, in our likeness designed.

He shaped them both from breath and
bone-to walk with Him, not stand alone.

And God blessed them and gave this command, to watch over His creation and increase in the land.

So, day six was complete. Trees, leaves, seeds and fruit so sweet, all created good for man and animals to eat.

By Day Seven, God's work was done,
the sea, the stars, Moon and Sun.

The sky above, the Earth below, the
birds that fly, the wind to blow.
A day for stillness, a day for rest.
He made it holy and called it blessed.

God spoke each part just as you've read, And all was made just as He said.

He looked with love at all He'd done, And saw it good- each single one.

So when you look at sky or tree, Or
Sun or Moon you plainly see.

Remember this, and hold it true:
The God who made it all loves you too.

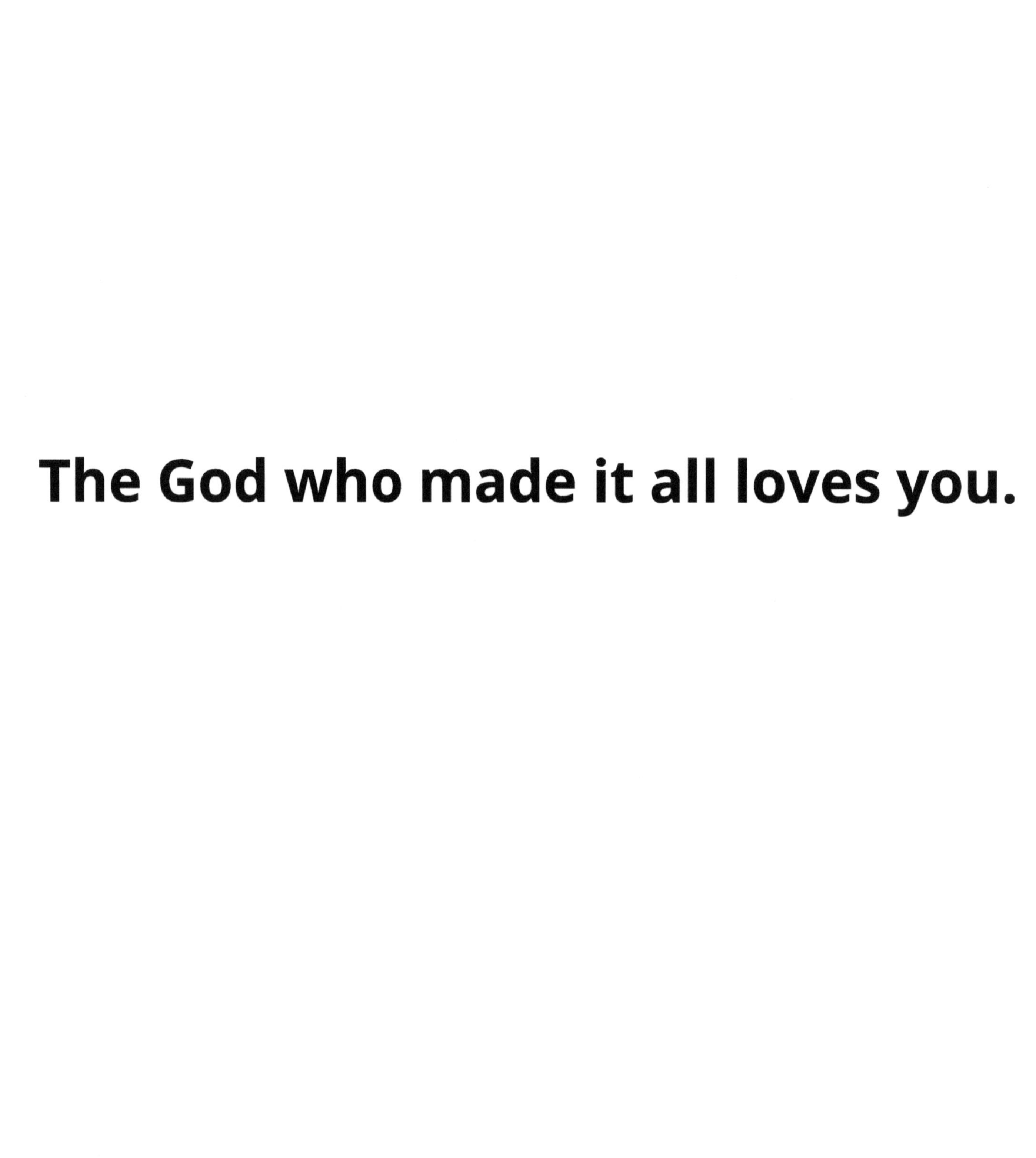

The God who made it all loves you.

A Note for Grown-ups

This book follows the Bible's account of how God created the world. It is meant to be read slowly, wondered about, and returned to again and again.

You don't need all the answers-just time together.
Here are some gentle questions you can ask after reading:

* Which day stood out to you the most?
* What did God say after each day was finished?
* What part of creation makes you feel thankful?
* How does it make you feel to know God made everything?
* What does it mean to you that God loves you?

www.ingramcontent.com/pod-product-compliance
Lightning Source LLC
Chambersburg PA
CBHW041949140726
48006CB00002BA/560